SUPER EASY SONGBOOK

Disney
THE LION KING

MUSIC FROM THE MOTION PICTURE SOUNDTRACK

ISBN 978-1-5400-6584-1

HAL•LEONARD®

Visit Hal Leonard Online at
www.halleonard.com

Contact us:
Hal Leonard
7777 West Bluemound Road
Milwaukee, WI 53213
Email: info@halleonard.com

In Europe, contact:
Hal Leonard Europe Limited
42 Wigmore Street
Marylebone, London, W1U 2RN
Email: info@halleonardeurope.com

In Australia, contact:
Hal Leonard Australia Pty. Ltd.
4 Lentara Court
Cheltenham, Victoria, 3192 Australia
Email: info@halleonard.com.au

Welcome to the *Super Easy Songbook* series!

This unique collection will help you play your favorite songs quickly and easily. Here's how it works:

- Play the simplified melody with your right hand. Letter names appear inside each note to assist you.

- There are no key signatures to worry about! If a sharp ♯ or flat ♭ is needed, it is shown beside the note each time.

- There are no page turns, so your hands never have to leave the keyboard.

- If two notes are connected by a tie ⌣, hold the first note for the combined number of beats. (The second note does not show a letter name since it is not re-struck.)

- Add basic chords with your left hand using the provided keyboard diagrams. Chord voicings have been carefully chosen to minimize hand movement.

- The left-hand rhythm is up to you, and chord notes can be played together or separately. Be creative!

- If the chords sound muddy, move your left hand an octave* higher. If this gets in the way of playing the melody, move your right hand an octave higher as well.

    * *An octave spans eight notes. If your starting note is C, the next C to the right is an octave higher.*

ALSO AVAILABLE

Hal Leonard Student Keyboard Guide HL00296039

Key Stickers HL00100016

Circle of Life

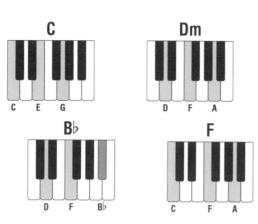
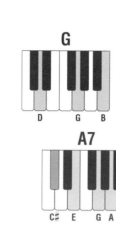
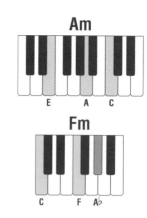

Music by Elton John
Lyrics by Tim Rice

Moderately

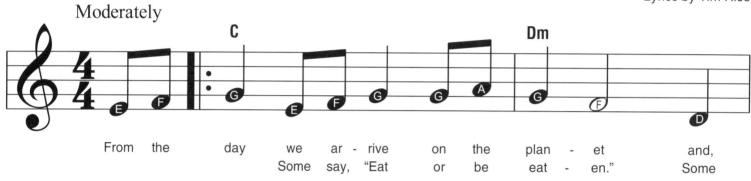

From the day we ar - rive on the plan - et and,
Some say, "Eat or be eat - en." and, Some

blink - ing, step in - to the sun, there's more to be seen than can
say, "Live and let live." But all are a - greed, as they

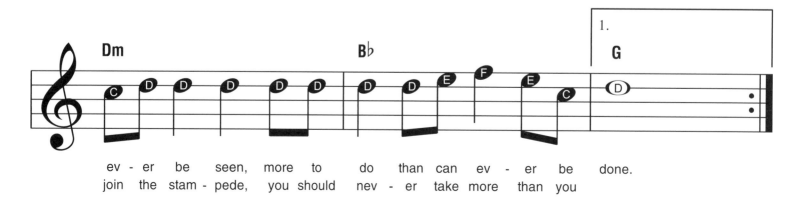

ev - er be seen, more to do than can ev - er be done.
join the stam - pede, you should nev - er take more than you

I Just Can't Wait to Be King

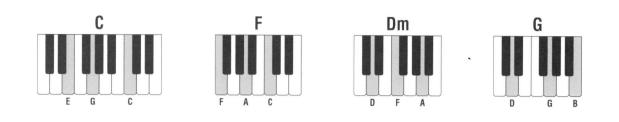

Music by Elton John
Lyrics by Tim Rice

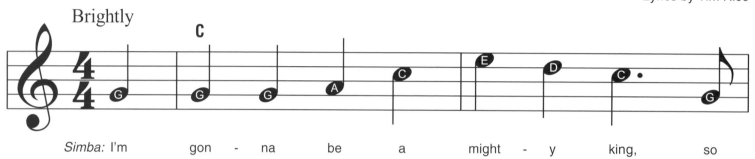

Simba: I'm gon - na be a might - y king, so

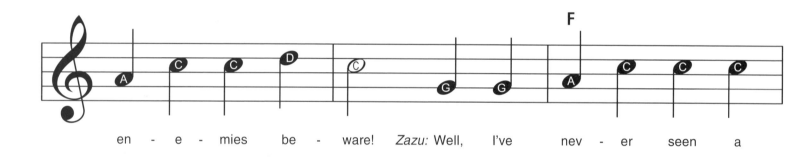

en - e - mies be - ware! Zazu: Well, I've nev - er seen a

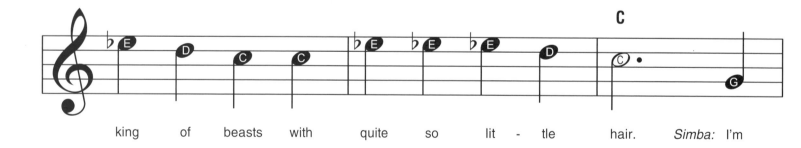

king of beasts with quite so lit - tle hair. Simba: I'm

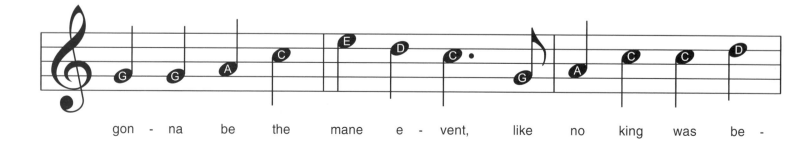

gon - na be the mane e - vent, like no king was be -

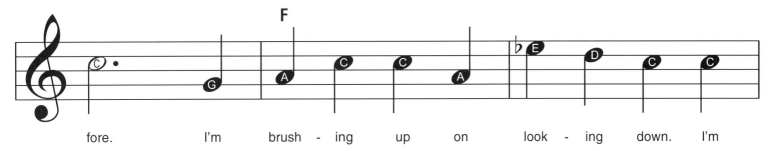

fore.   I'm   brush - ing   up   on   look - ing   down.   I'm

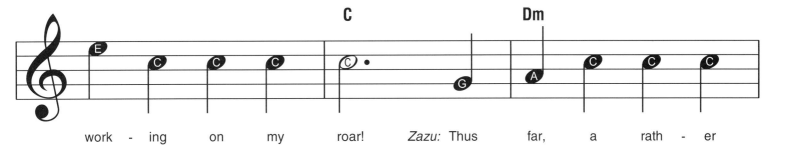

work - ing   on   my   roar!   *Zazu:* Thus   far,   a   rath - er

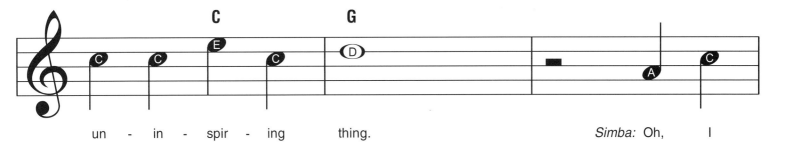

un - in - spir - ing   thing.   *Simba:* Oh,   I

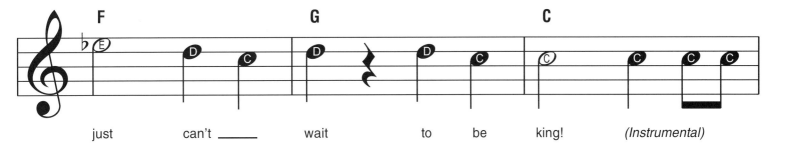

just   can't ____   wait   to   be   king!   *(Instrumental)*

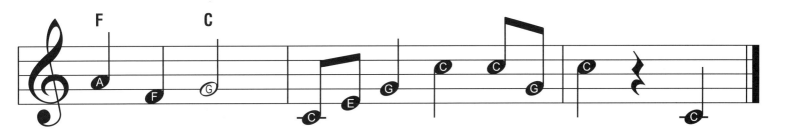

Be Prepared
(2019)

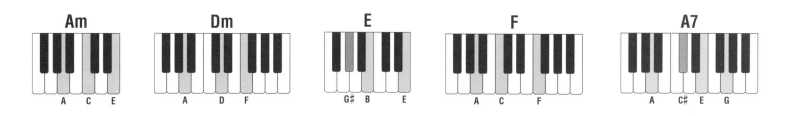

Music by Elton John
Lyrics by Tim Rice

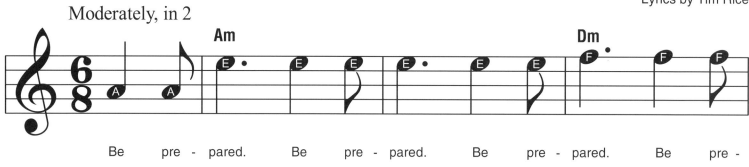

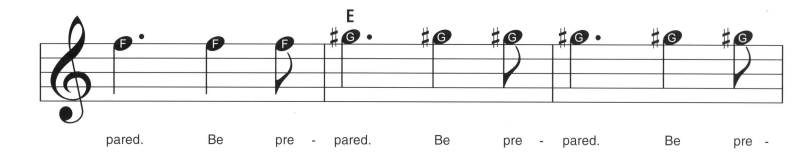

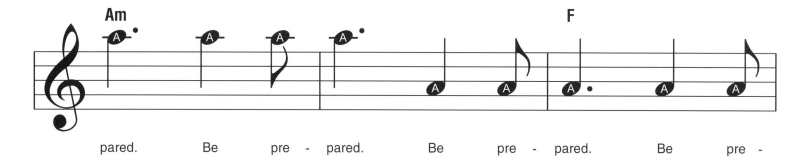

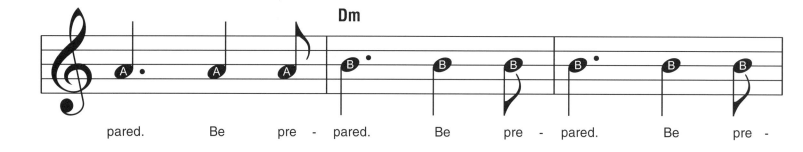

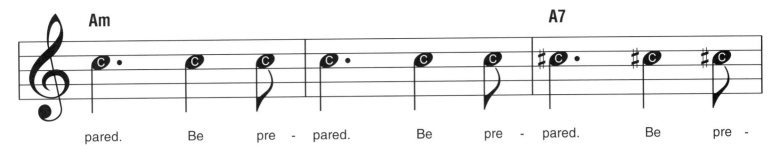

pared.   Be   pre - pared.   Be   pre - pared.   Be   pre -

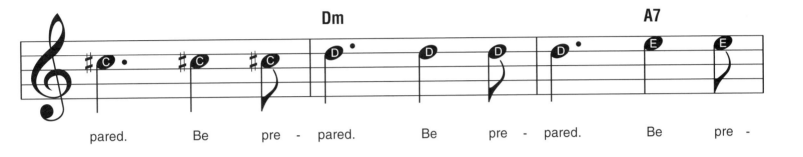

pared.   Be   pre - pared.   Be   pre - pared.   Be   pre -

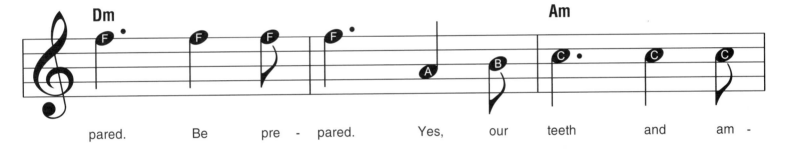

pared.   Be   pre - pared.   Yes,   our   teeth   and   am -

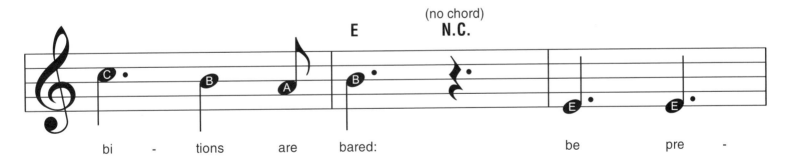

bi - tions   are   bared: be   pre -

pared. _____

Hakuna Matata

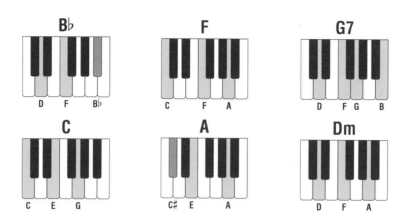

Music by Elton John
Lyrics by Tim Rice

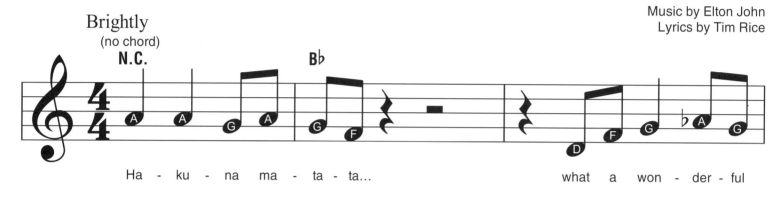

Ha - ku - na ma - ta - ta...   what a won - der - ful

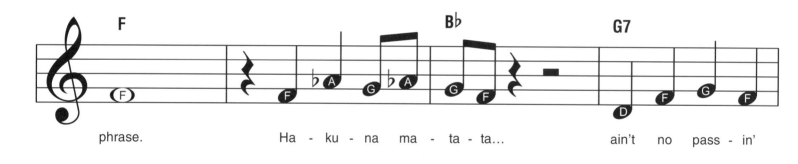

phrase.   Ha - ku - na ma - ta - ta...   ain't no pass - in'

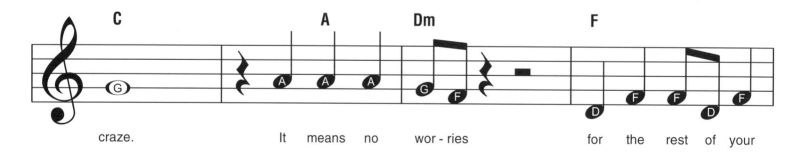

craze.   It means no wor - ries   for the rest of your

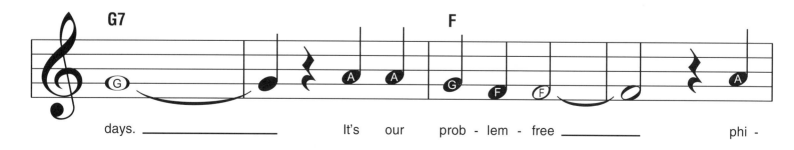

days. _____   It's our prob - lem - free _____ phi -

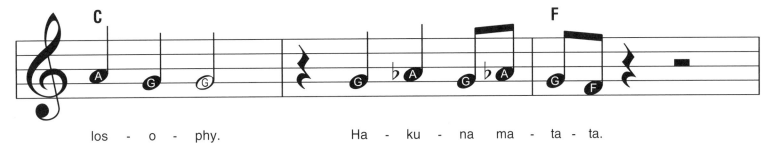

los - o - phy. Ha - ku - na ma - ta - ta.

Ha - ku - na ma - ta - ta... what a won - der - ful

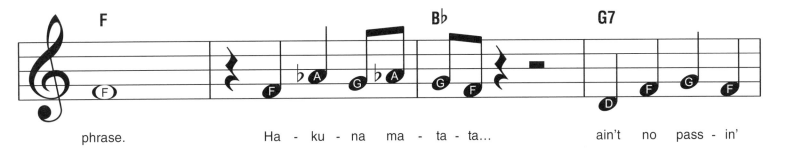

phrase. Ha - ku - na ma - ta - ta... ain't no pass - in'

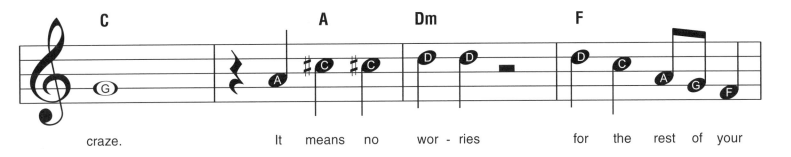

craze. It means no wor - ries for the rest of your

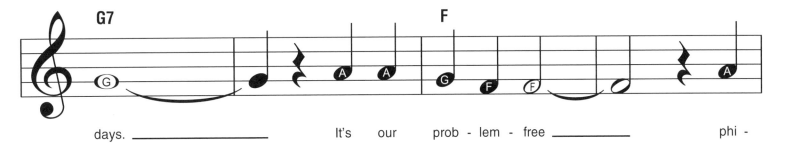

days. _____ It's our prob - lem - free _____ phi -

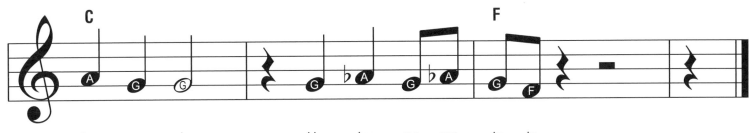

los - o - phy. Ha - ku - na ma - ta - ta.

The Lion Sleeps Tonight

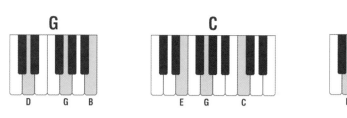

New Lyrics and Revised Music by George David Weiss,
Hugo Peretti and Luigi Creatore

Moderate Shuffle

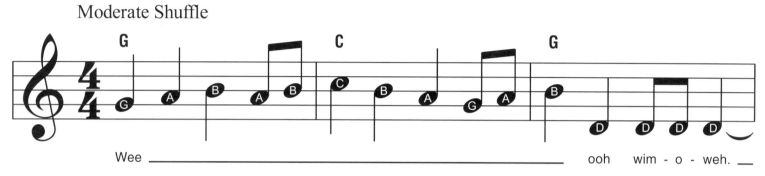

Wee _____ ooh wim - o - weh. __

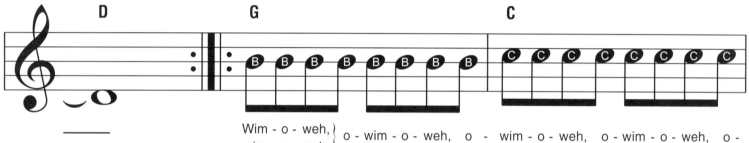

__ Wim - o - weh,⎫
wim - o - weh,⎭ o - wim - o - weh, o - wim - o - weh, o - wim - o - weh, o -

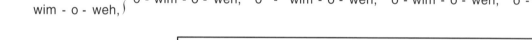

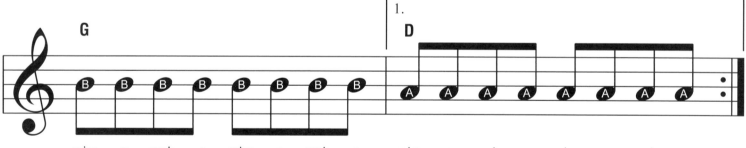

wim - o - weh, o - wim - o - weh, o - wim - o - weh, o - wim - o - weh, o -

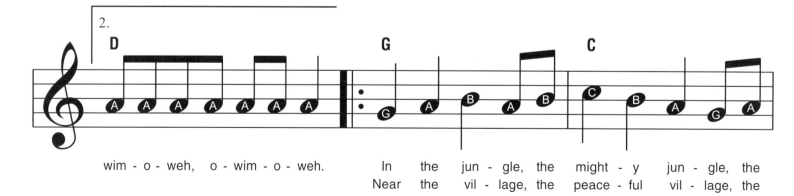

wim - o - weh, o - wim - o - weh. In the jun - gle, the might - y jun - gle, the
Near the vil - lage, the peace - ful vil - lage, the

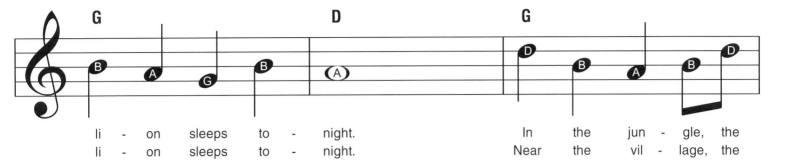

li - on sleeps to - night. In the jun - gle, the
li - on sleeps to - night. Near the vil - lage, the

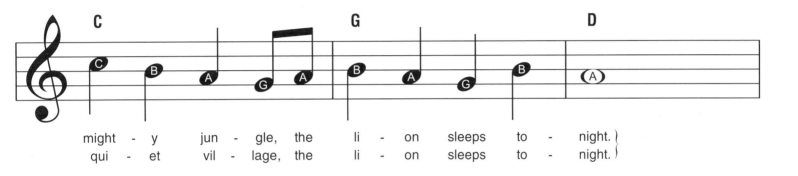

might - y jun - gle, the li - on sleeps to - night.
qui - et vil - lage, the li - on sleeps to - night.

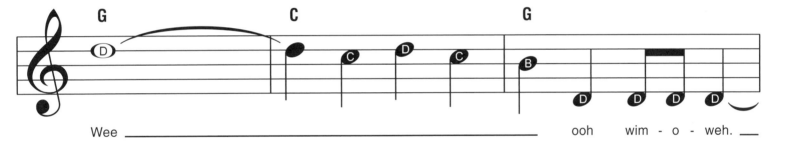

Wee _____ ooh wim - o - weh. ___

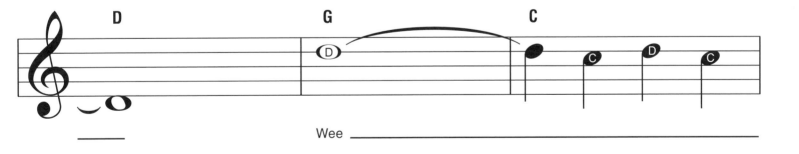

___ Wee _____

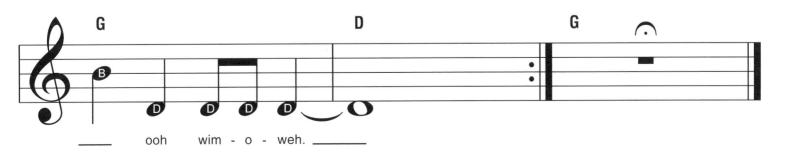

___ ooh wim - o - weh. _____

Can You Feel the Love Tonight

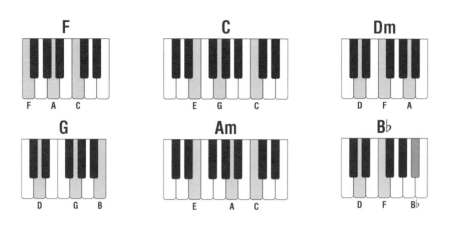

Music by Elton John
Lyrics by Tim Rice

Moderately slow

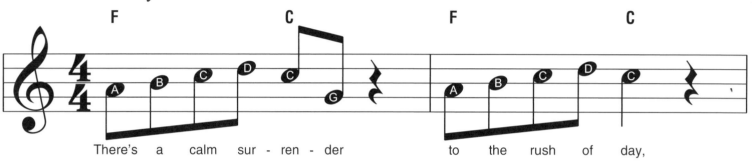

There's a calm sur - ren - der to the rush of day,

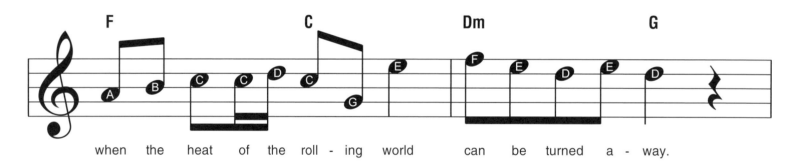

when the heat of the roll - ing world can be turned a - way.

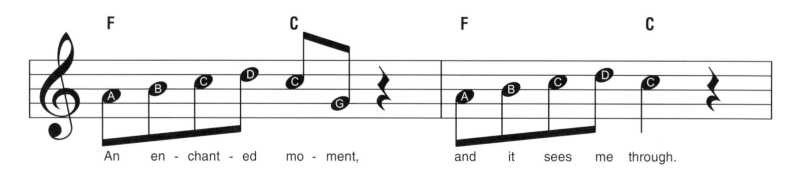

An en - chant - ed mo - ment, and it sees me through.

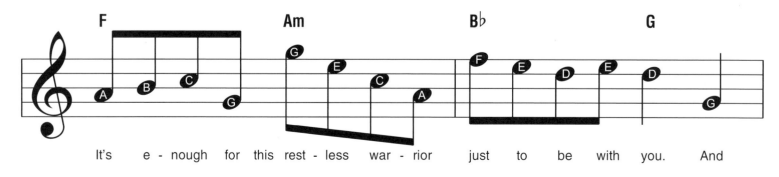

It's e - nough for this rest - less war - rior just to be with you. And

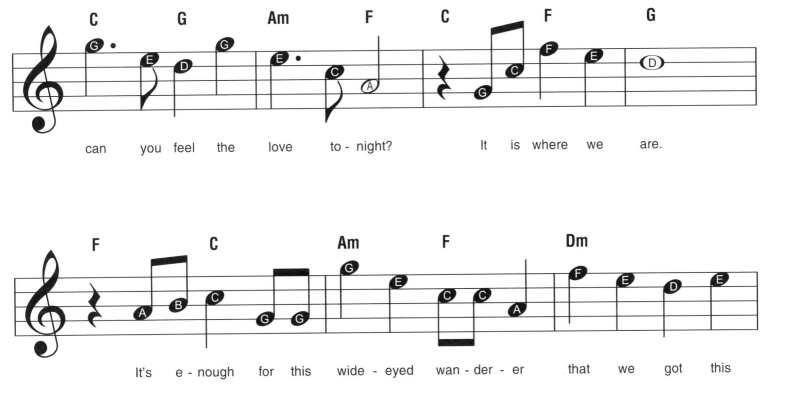

can you feel the love to - night? It is where we are.

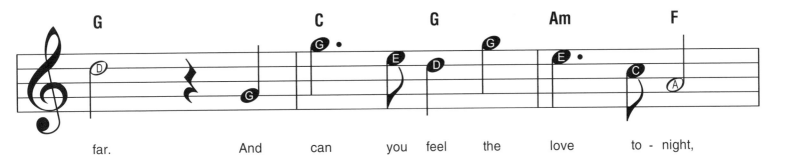

It's e - nough for this wide - eyed wan - der - er that we got this

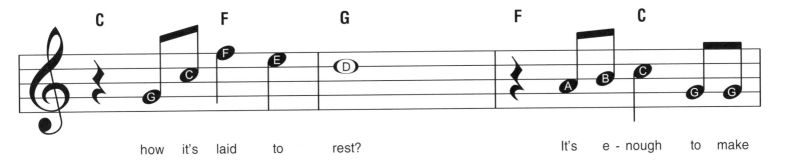

far. And can you feel the love to - night,

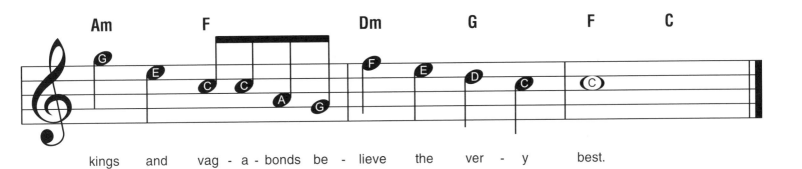

how it's laid to rest? It's e - nough to make

kings and vag - a - bonds be - lieve the ver - y best.

Spirit

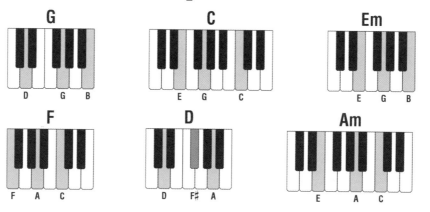

Written by Timothy McKenzie,
Ilya Salmanzadeh and Beyoncé

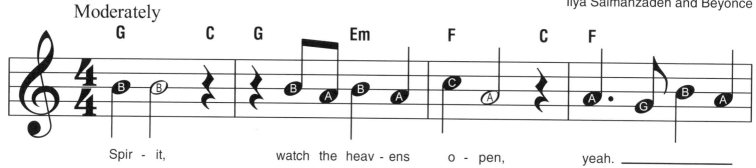

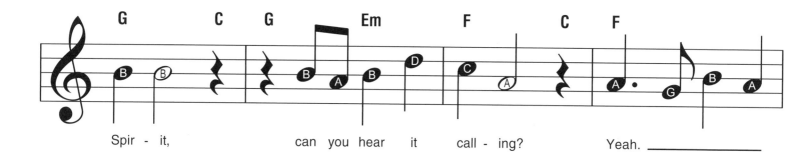

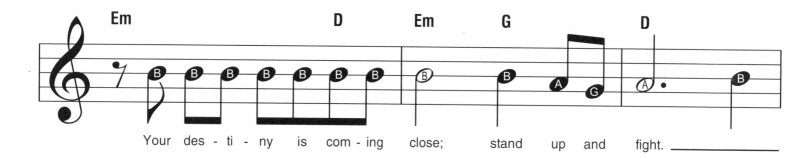

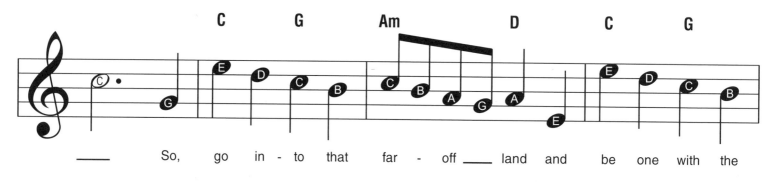

Never Too Late

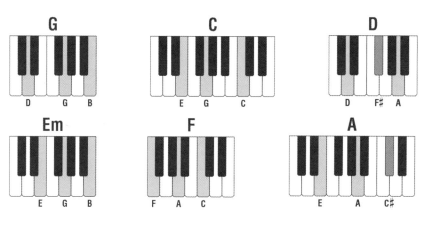

Music by Elton John
Lyrics by Tim Rice

Moderately fast

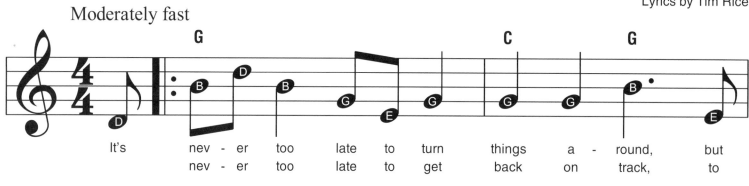

It's nev-er too late to turn things a-round, but
nev-er too late to get things back on track, to

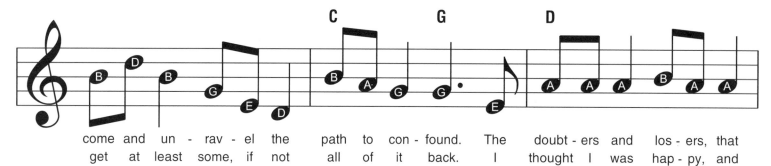

come and un-rav-el the path to con-found. The doubt-ers and los-ers, that
get at least some, if not all of it back. I thought I was hap-py, and

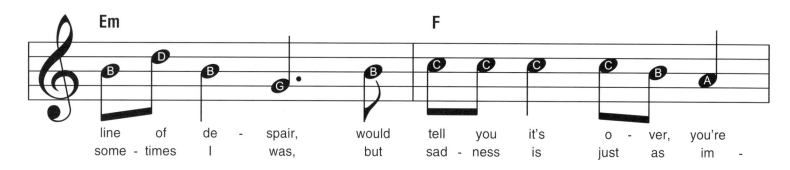

line of de-spair, would tell you it's o-ver, you're
some-times I was, but sad-ness is just as im-

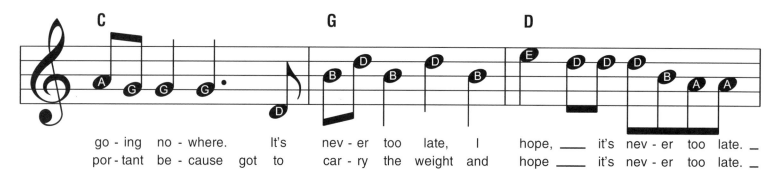

go-ing no-where. It's nev-er too late, I hope, ___ it's nev-er too late. ___
por-tant be-cause got to car-ry the weight and hope ___ it's nev-er too late. ___

He Lives in You

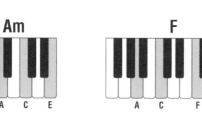
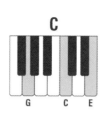
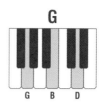

Lyrics and Music by Mark Mancina,
Jay Rifkin and Lebohang Morake

Moderately

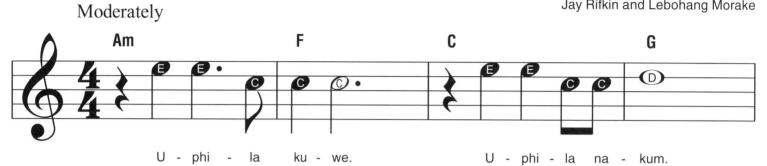

U - phi - la ku - we.   U - phi - la na - kum.

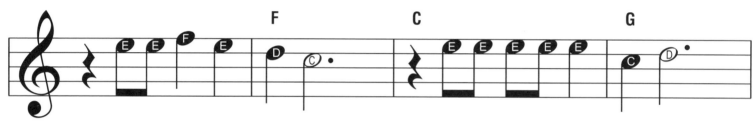

U - hla - l'e - jon - gi - le.   Yon - kin - to en - siyi - bo - na - yo.

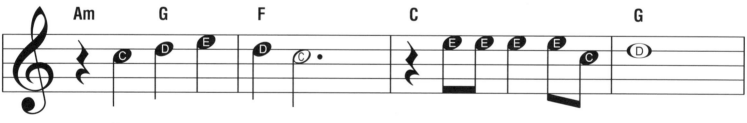

Nan - sene - man - zi - ni,   na - sen - ya - ni - swe - ni.

Na - se mfa - ne - ki - swe - ni wa - kho.   U - phi - la ku - we.

English Translation

He lives in you. He lives in me.
He watches over everything we see.
Into the water, into the truth,
In your reflection, he lives in you.
He lives in you.

It's super easy! This series features accessible arrangements for piano, with simple right-hand melody, letter names inside each note, and basic left-hand chord diagrams. Perfect for players of all ages!

THE BEATLES

All You Need Is Love • Come Together • Get Back • Here Comes the Sun • Hey Jude • I Want to Hold Your Hand • Let It Be • Something • We Can Work It Out • Yesterday • and many more.
00198161.. $14.99

BROADWAY

All I Ask of You • Bring Him Home • Cabaret • Dancing Queen • Edelweiss • Footloose • Hello, Dolly! • Memory • Ol' Man River • Seasons of Love • Try to Remember • and many more.
00193871.. $14.99

CHRISTMAS CAROLS

Away in a Manger • Coventry Carol • The First Noel • Go, Tell It on the Mountain • Jingle Bells • Joy to the World • O Holy Night • Silent Night • The Twelve Days of Christmas • and more.
00277955 .... $14.99

CHRISTMAS SONGS

All I Want for Christmas Is You • Do You Hear What I Hear • Frosty the Snow Man • Mary, Did You Know? • Rudolph the Red-Nosed Reindeer • Silver Bells • White Christmas • Winter Wonderland • and more.
00236850 .... $14.99

CLASSICAL

Canon (Pachelbel) • Für Elise (Beethoven) • Jesu, Joy of Man's Desiring • (J.S. Bach) • Lullaby (Brahms) • Pomp and Circumstance (Elgar) • Trumpet Voluntary (Clarke) • William Tell Overture (Rossini) • and many more.
00194693 .... $14.99

DISNEY

Be Our Guest • Chim Chim Cher-ee • A Dream Is a Wish Your Heart Makes • Friend like Me • Heigh-Ho • Kiss the Girl • Let It Go • A Spoonful of Sugar • When You Wish upon a Star • Winnie the Pooh • You've Got a Friend in Me • and more.
00199558 .... $14.99

FOUR CHORD SONGS

Beast of Burden • Careless Whisper • Despacito • Hey, Soul Sister • I'm a Believer • Jessie's Girl • Last Kiss • Let It Be • No Rain • Pink Houses • Run-Around • Stand by Me • Toes • Wagon Wheel • and many more.
00249533 .... $14.99

GOSPEL

Because He Lives • Give Me That Old Time Religion • How Great Thou Art • I Saw the Light • I'll Fly Away • The King Is Coming • The Old Rugged Cross • Precious Memories • Soon and Very Soon • and more.
00285256 .... $14.99

HIT SONGS

All of Me • Brave • Can't Feel My Face • Ex's & Oh's • Ho Hey • Jar of Hearts • Lost Boy • Riptide • Rolling in the Deep • Shake It Off • Stay with Me • A Thousand Years • and more.
00194367 .... $14.99

HYMNS

All Creatures of Our God and King • Amazing Grace • Be Thou My Vision • Crown Him with Many Crowns • For the Beauty of the Earth • I Love to Tell the Story • O Worship the King • Rock of Ages • We Gather Together • What a Friend We Have in Jesus • and many more.
00194659 .... $14.99

JAZZ STANDARDS

Body and Soul • Cheek to Cheek • Embraceable You • Georgia on My Mind • I Got Rhythm • The Nearness of You • Satin Doll • Someone to Watch over Me • The Way You Look Tonight • and more.
00233687 .... $14.99

KIDS' SONGS

"C" Is for Cookie • Do-Re-Mi • Electricity • I'm Popeye the Sailor Man • Over the Rainbow • Puff the Magic Dragon • The Rainbow Connection • Sesame Street Theme • Tomorrow • You Are My Sunshine • and many more.
00198009 .... $14.99

ANDREW LLOYD WEBBER

Any Dream Will Do • Buenos Aires • Don't Cry for Me Argentina • Love Never Dies • Memory • The Music of the Night • The Perfect Year • Superstar • Unexpected Song • Wishing You Were Somehow Here Again • and more.
00249580 .... $14.99

MOVIE SONGS

Chariots of Fire • City of Stars • Eye of the Tiger • Happy • Kiss from a Rose • Moon River • Over the Rainbow • Somewhere Out There • (I've Had) The Time of My Life • What a Wonderful World • and more.
00233670 .... $14.99

POP STANDARDS

Africa • Bridge over Troubled Water • Careless Whisper • Every Breath You Take • God Only Knows • Hallelujah • Just the Way You Are • Right Here Waiting • Stand by Me • Tears in Heaven • The Wind Beneath My Wings • You've Got a Friend • and many more.
00233770 .... $14.99

QUEEN

Another One Bites the Dust • Bohemian Rhapsody • Crazy Little Thing Called Love • Fat Bottomed Girls • I Want to Break Free • Radio Ga Ga • Somebody to Love • Under Pressure • and more.
00294889 .... $9.99

ED SHEERAN

The A Team • Castle on the Hill • Don't • Happier • I See Fire • Lego House • Perfect • Photograph • Shape of You • Sing • Thinking Out Loud • and more.
00287525 .... $9.99

THREE CHORD SONGS

All About That Bass • Beat It • Clocks • Evil Ways • Folsom Prison Blues • Hound Dog • Jolene • Kiss • La Bamba • Old Time Rock & Roll • Riptide • Twist and Shout • Use Somebody • Walk of Life • and more.
00249664 .... $14.99

WWW.HALLEONARD.COM